Dare
to DREAM

journal belongs to...

© 2016 Ranch House Press
All rights reserved. Printed in the United States of America.

www.annettebridges.com

ISBN: 978-0-9981576-2-7

Journal Prompts
Dare to DREAM

1. What are three things in your life that you would change if you could?
2. Dear future me... (Write a letter to your future self)
3. (Fill in the blank) If money, resources and health were not issues, I would...
4. What grand adventure do you want to go on someday?
5. What would your perfect day be like?
6. If you could become an expert in any subject or activity, what would it be?
7. What would you ask for if a genie granted you three wishes?
8. What are the top ten characteristics that you look for in a mate?
9. What's your secret desire that no one else knows?
10. How can you get more stillness, solitude and peace in your life?
11. What can you do to nurture your important relationships?
12. (Fill in the blank) I feel happiest when...
13. (Fill in the blank with a list of 50 things) I wish I could...
14. Describe the best night dream you can remember.
15. Some things you've never had but want.
16. Some things you've never done but want to.
17. Your ideal holiday or vacation would be...
18. (Fill in the blank) I want to learn more about...
19. What can you do to have more fun in your life?
20. (Fill in the blank) The words I'd like to live by are...
21. Make a list of things you want to do before next year.
22. Imagine yourself at a favorite location. Describe your experience, how you feel, what you're thinking, your field of vision.
23. Make a list of things you would like to know how to do.
24. Write a goal you have for your self, your relationships, your career/passion, your health. Then write three things that you can do to accomplish each goal.
25. Define "dream." Create a word bank. List synonymns.
26. What event on the horizon is making you anxious? In one sentence answer why. What's the worst thing that could happen? And the best? Come back after the event and write about what actually happened.
27. List five people and how you think they would describe you in one sentence. Next... ask them to describe you in one sentence and compare.
28. List things you don't have or haven't experienced before that you think will make you happier.
29. Reflect on your life so far and make a list of what you wish you spent more time on.
30. Reflect on your life so far and make a list of what you wish you have spent less time on.
31. Make a collage of what "calm" looks like to you.

color your world

ABOUT the CREATOR

Annette Bridges is an author, publisher and women's retreat host on a mission to help every woman realize her story is extraordinary, valuable and noteworthy.

She has published the ***Color Your World Journal Series*** and formed a journal club to provide community, support and tools for women to record their ideas, feelings, experiences, memories and all the important details of their lives.

Before writing books and publishing journals and coloring books, this former public school and homeschool educator spent a decade writing hundreds of helpful, instructive, and light-hearted columns published by Texas newspapers, parenting magazines, websites and bloggers.

Annette lives on a Texas cattle ranch with her husband John, dachshund Lady and lots of cows. She can drive a tractor but only if wearing a fresh coat of lipstick and it's not her pedicure day!

You can learn more about Annette's books and products, blogs and videos as well as her women's retreats and other events at www.annettebridges.com.

Look for her on social media, too!

MESSAGE from the PUBLISHER

The *Color Your World Journal Series* is a pathway to self-discovery. It's where you write notes to yourself. Be your own cheerleader. Give yourself encouragement. Tell yourself what you're grateful for. Celebrate you!

There are countless reasons to keep a journal including collecting favorite recipes, listing goals and celebrating every experience and every one that's near and dear to you. A journal provides a home for the memories and lessons learned that you never want to forget.

Why a niche journal?

If you're anything like me, you have a journal (or even two or three journals) where you write anything and everything about anything and everything. My challenge comes when trying to find something I've written. I flip and flip through the pages of my two, three or four journals trying to find whatever it is. I never remember which journal I wrote down my whatever's!!

The solution? A niche journal! A journal that has a specific focus and theme! A journal where you can record your ideas, inspirations and things you want to remember in the appropriate journal.

Why big unlined paper?

Because big unlined paper is needed to record big ideas, dreams and memories! You need room to grow, stretch and expand. You need space to think beyond the confines of what you've always done, to pursue new dreams, discover your power and reimagine your purpose again and again. You need pages without lines and limitations to reconnect with your creative, perfectly imperfect self.

Plus, big unlined paper gives you space for more than words. You have plenty of room to doodle, draw or post photographs and clippings, too.

Why color is important?

When you journal, use colored pens and markers! Your world doesn't happen in black and white. Your life should be lived and written about in many colors. Even dark and sad memories feel lighter and brighter when told in color.

Journaling in color affects your mood and perception of your world. Colors evoke calm, cheer and comfort. Using color can lift your spirit and inspire your imagination. You may be surprised by all the beautiful benefits from adding more color into your life story.

When journaling, give yourself time to listen to your heart and reflect. Breathe in the moments. Feel. Be quiet. Let yourself be totally and thoroughly present with your thoughts. Let your heart transform you and teach you new insights. Open your mind to consider new ideas and possibilities. You may find that what your heart teaches will be life changing.

www.ingramcontent.com/pod-product-compliance
Lightning Source LLC
Chambersburg PA
CBHW061933290426
44113CB00024B/2900